Original title:
Leaves of Laughter

Copyright © 2025 Creative Arts Management OÜ
All rights reserved.

Author: Vivian Laurent
ISBN HARDBACK: 978-1-80567-190-9
ISBN PAPERBACK: 978-1-80567-489-4

Whispers of Joyful Breezes

In the park, a duck did waddle,
Chasing kids, but staying subtle.
Laughter bursts from every smile,
As giggles dance and stretch a mile.

Squirrels tease with acorn games,
Jumping high with silly names.
The sunbeams play an endless tune,
While shadows twirl, all afternoon.

Petals of Playfulness

Daisies giggle, swaying low,
Whisper secrets to the flow.
Butterflies in fancy dress,
Flutter past in pure excess.

A puppy chases its own tail,
Around the path where echoes hail.
With silly jumps, it makes a fuss,
It's hard not to simply trust.

Giggles in the Grove

Underneath the arching trees,
A gathering of happy bees.
They buzz along with playful grins,
As nature joins in on the spins.

The creek bubbles with a laugh,
As pebbles form a fun-filled path.
Each splash is met with cheer and jest,
Painting joy for every guest.

Merriment Under the Canopy

In the shade, the children play,
Chasing shadows all the way.
Their laughter echoes through the leaves,
As the warm breeze gently weaves.

A frog croaks jokes, so loud and clear,
Making all the critters leer.
With every leap, they share a grin,
In this fun-filled world, we spin.

Giggling Under the Canopy of Colors

Beneath bright branches, we frolic free,
Colors dance, as silly as can be.
A tickle of wind, a playful tease,
Nature chuckles, putting us at ease.

Squirrels dart with acorns, a playful game,
While birds whistle tunes, calling our name.
The sun shines down, casting cheeky rays,
As we twirl and spin in a whimsical haze.

The Ecstasy of Nature's Jest

In fields of joy, the daisies grin,
Their petals whisper secrets from within.
Butterflies flutter, a frolicsome band,
Their colors a jester, oh how they stand!

Rabbits hop in a giddy ballet,
Chasing shadows that dance and sway.
The brook burbles laughter, a melody sweet,
Nature's own joker, never discreet.

Serene Smiles of Flora and Fauna

The flowers giggle in hues so bright,
Inviting us into their playful sight.
Bees buzz round with a mischievous glee,
Gathering sweetness, so carefree.

A frog on a lily, croaks with delight,
As fireflies twinkle, lighting the night.
The grasses sway in a jovial dance,
Encouraging all with a merry glance.

When Nature Breaks into Song

In the hush of dawn, birds start to chirp,
Their melodies weave a playful burp.
A rustle of leaves, the wind joins in,
A symphony of joy, where laughter begins.

The branches sway with a gentle laugh,
As sunlight plays upon the path.
Nature's jokes, wrapped in each sound,
Wrapping us in joy profound.

The Giggle of the Golden Foliage

Golden hues dance in the breeze,
Wiggling whimsies in the trees.
Each rustle a chuckle, each flip a jest,
Nature's humor at its best.

A squirrel in shades of bright delight,
Chasing shadows, what a sight!
With every turn, a silly play,
Glee spills forth in golden array.

Joy Unfurled in Nature's Embrace

Crisp air filled with chuckle and cheer,
Happiness whispers, 'Come dance near!'
Bouncing branches, a playful sway,
Nature's laughter brightens the day.

The flowers giggle in colors bold,
Each petal a story, a secret told.
In the arms of earth, we twirl and spin,
Joy's a dance, let the fun begin!

The Melody of Mirthful Winds

Winds play tunes on branches high,
Tickling leaves as they flutter by.
A melody bright, a symphony sly,
Nature's jest, oh my, oh my!

With every gust, a playful tease,
Whirling whispers through the trees.
Resounding giggles in the air,
Come join the fun, if you dare!

Fable of the Merry Petals

In gardens where the laughter grows,
Blooming tales that nobody knows.
Petals dance, a whimsical flair,
Each blush and giggle fills the air.

From daffodils to the shyest rose,
Every bloom in quirky pose.
Nature's jesters, bold and bright,
Spreading joy, a pure delight.

Revelations in the Rustling Roots

In whispers deep where roots conspire,
The ants debate, what's funnier? Sire!
A worm winks slyly, a joke unfolds,
As giggles rise from the soil untold.

The grass blades sway, they chuckle too,
At the gossiping breeze, oh what a view!
With giggles tickling each dew-kissed leaf,
Nature's jesters, bringing forth relief.

They swirl and twirl in earthy jest,
A dance of humor, nature's best,
A squirrel cracks jokes on a branch above,
Making all around feel the warmth of love.

The Cheer of Blossoms Unfolding

Petals flutter, a lively cheer,
The flowers gossip, lend an ear!
"Oh look, the sun is a jester bright,
Tickling our colors, a marvelous sight!"

Bumblebees buzz with a happy tune,
As daisies dance beneath the moon,
"Did you hear the rose's latest claim?
She says she's the star of the plant-based game!"

Tulips chuckle in polka-dot coats,
While lilacs tease in their lilting quotes,
In this bloom-filled jest, laughter reigns,
Colorful joy in the garden's veins.

Jests in a Treetop Tea Party

High in the branches, a party goes,
Where acorns chatter, and humor flows.
"A cup of nectar, a jest, a laugh,
Let's toast to the squirrel, our comedic half!"

The bluebirds chirp with witty replies,
As chipmunks tell tales of the night skies,
"Did you see how the owl tripped and fell?
He landed right near a laughing bell!"

With laughter and songs in the leafy air,
Nature's tea party, free of a care,
In this tree-top realm, humor takes flight,
As giggles cascade into the soft night.

Warmth Wrapped in Nature's Tapestry

In the sun's embrace, the world feels bright,
A tapestry woven, a funny sight.
"Did you hear the joke from the old oak tree?
He's been telling it since 'ninety-three!'"

The clouds drift by with a smirk and a grin,
As they tickle the hills, where chuckles begin,
Each rustle of leaves, a chorus of fun,
In this warmth wrapped tight 'neath the playful sun.

Laughter echoing in every vale,
As flowers burst forth, a joyful tale,
With smiles aplenty, life's a great song,
In nature's embrace, where we all belong.

The Hum of Happy Moments

Bouncing like balls in the air,
Laughter echoes here and there.
Each chuckle tickles the bright sun,
Jokes are traded, just for fun.

Giggling ants in a parade,
Wobbly squirrels join the charade.
With each quip, the world turns light,
Joy ignites, banishing night.

Brightness Between Branches

A playful breeze makes the trees sway,
Whispers of giggles dance and play.
Sunlight filtering, a golden tease,
Nature's laughter rustles the leaves.

Silly shadows stretch and leap,
In sunny patches where giggles seep.
Hopping hearts and grinning faces,
Life's a joke in these green places.

Revelry Among the Verdant Veils

Beneath the canopy, glee unfolds,
Stories of mischief and laughter told.
All creatures come for a blissful spree,
Celebrating life under a fig tree.

Frogs wear crowns, and snails take a bow,
The cheerful chaos calls us now.
With each footfall, the fun grows strong,
In this wild revelry, we all belong.

Playful Whispers of the Wild

Gentle nudges in the soft grass,
Giggling critters in a lively mass.
Butterflies dance with fluttering grace,
Their antics bring smiles to every face.

In every rustle, a chuckle shared,
Nature's humor, beautifully paired.
Witty blooms in colors so bright,
The wild whispers of pure delight.

Joyful Murmurs of Nature

Whispers dance on branches high,
Silly echoes, birds that fly.
Bouncing rocks with playful glee,
Nature's jesters, wild and free.

Tickling blooms that sway and grin,
Sunlight's laughter, soft within.
Wiggling worms in muddy play,
Giggling at the end of day.

Uplifted Spirits in the Wild

Swaying grass with joyful spright,
Bugs doing dances, oh what a sight!
Frisky foxes prance around,
In the meadow's merry sound.

Bubbling brooks in jestful leap,
Nature's humor, lush and deep.
Cheerful clouds in silly chase,
Tickled skies with smiling face.

Breezy Chuckles

Windy whispers tease the trees,
Laughter carried on the breeze.
Dancing petals tease the ground,
Joyful music all around.

Rustling leaves in playful tease,
Tiny critters scurry with ease.
Sunset brings a funny glow,
Nature's show, a carnival.

The Tickle of the Trees

Branches bend with cheeky grace,
Breezy giggles fill the space.
Squirrels chatter, jokes to share,
While shadows play without a care.

Whimsical winds that swirl and sway,
Sing to brighten up the day.
In this realm of happy glee,
Nature wraps us joyfully.

In the Company of Merry Mirages

In the garden of giggles, I stroll,
Where daisies whisper secrets, oh so droll.
Butterflies tease the bumblebees,
While the sun chuckles through the trees.

Rabbits wearing hats bounce around,
Telling jokes that seldom make a sound.
The breeze plays tricks, a playful tease,
As I dance along with joy and ease.

Frogs in tuxedos croak a tune,
Making frogs laugh beneath the moon.
The flowers blush in colors bright,
Painting smiles that bloom with delight.

Here in mirage, where silliness reigns,
Life's a circus, where joy never wanes.
In every nook, laughter takes flight,
A harmonious chaos, pure delight.

The Comedy of Nature's Palette

Sunflowers wink with a golden grin,
Cheerful daisies join in with a spin.
Crickets chirp in rhythm and rhyme,
As nature crafts laughter, every time.

Squirrels play acrobat, flip and twirl,
Chasing each other in a wild whirl.
Leaves chuckle softly in the breeze,
Tickled pink by nature's antics with ease.

Puddles giggle with splashes loud,
As raindrops leap, oh so proud.
Trees put on hats made of shade,
Wardrobe of whispers, nature's parade.

Jokes are written on the sky in hues,
A canvas of joy, happy news.
Here's to the chuckles that never fade,
In nature's comedy, where dreams are made.

Cascades of Cheerful Sighs

The river sings with a bubbly flow,
Telling tales only fishes know.
Pebbles giggle as they tumble down,
Wearing water hats, no sign of frown.

Clouds drift lazily, puffed with glee,
Dancing like cotton, wild and free.
While rain starts playing leapfrog with the sun,
A game of hide and seek, oh, what fun!

In the breeze, laughter takes a bow,
With whispers of joy, oh so vivid now.
A symphony of chuckles in every sigh,
Nature's blend of bliss, oh my, oh my!

With every flutter, cheer cascades,
In the wilds of wonder, no charades.
Here's to a world where giggles collide,
In cheerful sighs, our hearts abide.

The Jests of Nature's Palette

Colors of mirth paint the skies,
With sunsets bringing giggling hi-fives.
Trees lean in, sharing jokes with the crows,
Nature's stand-up, where humor flows.

Mountains chuckle, rooted and stout,
While rivers chuckle, dancing about.
The sun casts shadows, a playful game,
In the theater of life, laughter's the name.

Cacti wear flowers, crowns of delight,
While lizards wear smiles, oh, what a sight!
In this jesting realm, joy does prevail,
As laughter echoes through the vale.

So gather round, let's celebrate cheer,
In the jest of nature, it's all so clear.
With every twist and tickle, we sing,
In the comedy of earth, joy's the king.

Frolics Along the Forest Floor

Beneath the trees, the squirrels race,
Chasing shadows, a wild embrace.
With acorn hats, they leap and twirl,
In the grand play of a nutty whirl.

The mushrooms giggle, wiggle, and sway,
As bunnies hop on a sunny day.
With every bounce, a chuckle spreads,
Nature's jesters, no worries or dreads.

Giddy Sprites in the Glade

Tiny sprites dance on breezy wings,
Twirling and whirling in joyful flings.
They tickle the flowers, much to their glee,
As petals shimmer with pure jubilee.

They hide in the ferns, giggling away,
Playing tricks on the bees who obey.
Spin and stumble, oh what a sight,
In the heart of the woods, pure delight!

Sunlit Stories of Delight

In golden rays, the laughter gleams,
Talking trees share rib-tickling dreams.
A fox in spectacles reads a tale,
Of mischief and joy that will never pale.

The butterflies paint the sky broad,
With colors that leave the world awed.
In every giggle, there's magic to find,
Stories of fun, with no limits defined.

Whimsy in the Woodland

Frogs in bow ties croak a tune,
Performing shows beneath the moon.
The owls hoot jokes, wise and spry,
While raccoons applaud, oh my, oh my!

In a patch of moss, a party brews,
With ants serving snacks and playful views.
Every nook hums with laughter and cheer,
In this wild woodland, fun is always near.

Serenade of Laughter

In the park where giggles bloom,
Jokes hide behind the trees' bright plume.
Silly winds carry whispers near,
Tickling ears with joy and cheer.

A jester hops, a clown does sway,
Bouncing jokes along the way.
The sun beams down with a grin,
As chuckles rise, let glee begin.

Puppy prances, tail held high,
Chasing shadows that flit by.
Every bark a punchline bright,
Sparkling through the day and night.

So let us sing this merry song,
In the company where we belong.
For laughter is the sweetest sound,
In every corner, joy is found.

Glee in the Glade

In a glade where the sprites collide,
Laughter bubbles, as if they hide.
With leaps and bounds, they play and soar,
For every giggle opens doors.

Pies in the sky and clouds that spin,
Cheesy puns where laughter begins.
The breeze meanders, whispers in tune,
Dance with joy beneath the moon.

Frisky squirrels toss acorns high,
Each one sent with a sparkling sigh.
They twirl and twist, a playful feast,
Provoking giggles, never the least.

So gather round in the glade of glee,
Let's tip our hats to jubilee.
With every chuckle, life's milder side,
Creating magic we cannot hide.

Dancing Shadows of Delight

Underneath the cover of trees,
Shadows dance with a gentle breeze.
Tickled pink with every sway,
Twisting tales in a playful way.

Bumblebees buzz a merry beat,
As flowers chuckle at passing feet.
Each petal flutters, all in jest,
In this haven, we find our rest.

Puppets of whimsy, they twirl and swoon,
Under the watch of a cheeky moon.
Every critter joins the parade,
In this ballet of joy carefully made.

So let us laugh, let our spirits rise,
As shadows twirl, beneath bright skies.
For each echo of joy in flight,
Is the essence of dancing delight.

Mirth in the Meadow

In meadows wide, where daisies play,
Joyful hearts skip through the day.
Laughter flows like a bubbling stream,
Filling the air with a sunny dream.

Tiny birds tweet in silly chirps,
While rabbits hop with playful jerks.
Frolicsome friends join the spree,
Creating a world that's wild and free.

Pies hilariously thrown with cheer,
A whipped cream fight, now don't you sneer!
Every giggle a spark in the green,
Mirth shines bright in this vibrant scene.

So dance and twirl, don't hold back,
In this meadow, we find our crack.
For in this bliss, we all belong,
Where laughter echoes—life's sweet song.

Smiles on the Wind

Breezes giggle through the trees,
Carrying chuckles with such ease.
Sunshine tickles every face,
In this merry, vibrant space.

Dancing petals swirl around,
Jokes of nature, light and sound.
Grasshoppers play their silly tune,
As daisies wink beneath the moon.

Birds exchange their silly calls,
While butterflies play hide and shawls.
Every branch a stage to spark,
Laughter echoes in the park.

Joyful whispers fill the air,
Life's a joke we all can share.
With each rustle, giggles bloom,
In the warmth of nature's room.

Nature's Playful Palette

Colors splash with a hearty cheer,
Every shade brings laughter near.
Purple blooms wear silly hats,
As hummingbirds do funny taps.

Roses wink with velvety eyes,
Underneath the sunny skies.
Each petal tells a joke in bloom,
Nature chuckles, taking room.

Caterpillars with dancing dreams,
Paint the world with giggling schemes.
Every pebble gets a grin,
Swirling joy where smiles begin.

Sunsets play with fiery flair,
As laughter lingers in the air.
Nature's brush, so bright and bold,
Creates a scene that's pure and gold.

Whispers of Joyful Breezes

Breezes whisper funny tales,
Tickling ears like gentle gales.
Clouds pay jokes in cotton fluff,
Rolling laughter, never tough.

Squirrels dance in comedic strides,
While the river chuckles and glides.
Every raindrop shares a grin,
As puddles fill with giggly din.

Sunrise paints the sky with cheer,
As flowers blossom, crystal clear.
With every gust, a joyful reign,
Laughter echoes like a train.

As shadows stretch and play around,
Nature's laughter knows no bound.
Each moment a merry disguise,
In the whispers of surprise.

The Dance of Playful Shadows

Shadows swirl in a lively dance,
Twisting, twirling, take a chance.
Each flicker tells a secret jest,
In the sunlight, they are at best.

Bouncing balls and giggly trails,
Nature's humor never fails.
Every corner hides a grin,
As laughter drifts, the fun begins.

Leaves chuckle in the playful air,
As shadows jump without a care.
Frolicking in the fading light,
Creating stories day and night.

Underneath these joyful hues,
Nature sings its silly blues.
Join the dance, let worries cease,
In the rhythm of sweet release.

Sunshine and Smiles Entwined

In the glow of the morning sun,
Giggles chase the day, oh what fun!
Joyful shadows jump and play,
Tickling secrets stir the way.

With whispers carried by the breeze,
Nature's jest, oh how it teases!
Bouncing blooms with hearts alight,
Roaring laughter fills the night.

Bubbles break in the warm air,
Every grin a little dare.
Silly dances spin around,
Chirping bravely, joy is found.

Underneath the golden glow,
Witty banter flows and grows.
Every twirl a splash of cheer,
Sunshine sparkles, smiles appear.

Riddles in the Rustling Treetops

Whispers rustle up high above,
A squirrel shares a tale of love.
Jokes hang like ripe fruit, so sweet,
Tickled branches sway in beat.

Oh, can you hear the dappled giggles?
Waving leaves share clever wiggles.
Each creature breathes a jest or two,
Witty secrets drift anew.

Up in branches, a chorus springs,
Funny echoes, laughter rings.
Jokes collide like clouds and light,
Crafting joy from day to night.

Nature's humor dances right,
With every flutter, pure delight.
Riddles weave through playful stories,
As laughter paints the world with glories.

When Light Meets Levity

Sunbeams dangle like golden threads,
Whisking worries, lifting heads.
Each glimmer plays a playful part,
Sparking joy from the heart.

In the garden where chuckles bloom,
Funny faces dispel the gloom.
Hummingbirds buzz, a banner of cheer,
As laughter dances, bright and clear.

Shadows frolic, leap, and twine,
Daily mischief in every line.
Giggly groups of critters play,
Making merriment of the day.

As sunshine dips and winks goodbye,
A chorus of chuckles fill the sky.
Light meets laughter, hand in hand,
Creating joy across the land.

Glee Adrift in the Forest

Bouncing beams through branches sway,
Giddy giggles lead the way.
Merry moments on every path,
Nature's whimsy stirs the laugh.

Morning light in playful bursts,
Tickling ferns and quenching thirsts.
Witty signs along the trail,
Serve up fun, let laughter sail.

Squirrels dance, not one bit shy,
Making merry as they fly.
With every rustle, joy erupts,
A wild world where glee instructs.

As the forest revels in jest,
Every creature knows its quest.
In this haven, smiles take flight,
Glee adrift from morn to night.

Radiance of Rapture

Sunshine tickles the trees,
Branches sway with glee,
Squirrels dance with delight,
While birds chirp in flight.

Breezes blow merry tunes,
Nature hums and croons,
Jokes hidden in the shade,
Laughter's serenade.

Whispers from the grass,
Witty wisecracks pass,
A world of silly pranks,
Filled with giggling thanks.

In this vibrant scene,
Life's a playful dream,
Joy blooms all around,
In laughter we are bound.

Frolics in the Foliage

Wiggly worms in a race,
Tickled by every pace,
Bunnies hop on the scene,
With antics so obscene.

Frisky foxes chase their tails,
While the wind tells funny tales,
A giggle in every glade,
Where silliness won't fade.

The trees wear playful hats,
As chipmunks chat with bats,
Nature's jesters all around,
Creating laughter sound.

With each rustle in the leaves,
A cheerful spirit weaves,
Frolics in sun's embrace,
Putting smiles on each face.

Harmony of the Heart

Joyful twirls through the air,
A harmony so rare,
Chirping frogs in a band,
Together they all stand.

Nature's giggles unite,
Bouncing high in the light,
Each bloom a silly grin,
In this world, we all win.

Whimsical winds softly sigh,
As butterflies drift by,
Every creature's in tune,
Laughing under the moon.

Heartbeats dance in delight,
Under stars shining bright,
In this playful embrace,
Laughter's warm, sweet grace.

Jests in the Jungle

Monkeys swinging in jest,
Turn the trees to a quest,
Parrots crack jokes aloud,
In a riotous crowd.

Tigers wear silly wigs,
While hippos do a jig,
The jungle bursts with mirth,
A carnival of birth.

Cheetahs running in glee,
Caught in pure jubilee,
Lemurs spin with pure flair,
In this laughter-filled air.

Echoes of joy resound,
In the wild, we are found,
Where each whimsy ignites,
And the spirit delights.

The Radiance of Joyful Shadows

In a world where whispers giggle,
Sunbeams play hide and seek with trees.
Laughter drips like summer drizzle,
While shadows dance, as light agrees.

A squirrel rolls in laughter's embrace,
Chasing dreams with acorn delight.
With silly grins upon its face,
It tumbles and twirls in the light.

Breezes chuckle through the boughs,
Tickling branches, oh what a tease!
Nature's humor, let's take a bow,
For each chuckle bends the knees.

In every rustle, a grin appears,
With joy that can't be held inside.
So let us dance away our fears,
In laughter's glow, forever tied.

Happy Trails Through the Grove

Strolling paths where giggles bloom,
Joyful echoes fill the air.
Every step dispels the gloom,
With each turn, laughter's flair.

Mushrooms wearing tiny hats,
Bow to travelers with ease.
A winking toad sings to the bats,
As butterflies sway like the breeze.

Chirps of crickets join the song,
A symphony of pure delight.
Nature's chorus, smooth and strong,
Guides us through the playful night.

In this grove where laughter grows,
Every heart becomes a drum.
With every chuckle, joy bestows,
A rhythm that we all become.

The Tenderness of Ticklish Tides

Waves that chuckle on the shore,
Tickling toes and whistling through.
The ocean's heart, it longs for more,
In playful tones, it hums its tune.

Seagulls laugh with beaks held high,
Surfboards dance upon the swell.
Splashing joy with every sigh,
In salty tales, the stories dwell.

Sandcastles giggle as they rise,
With crabs scuttling in a race.
Underneath the sunny skies,
There's nothing but a smiling face.

As the tide returns, we sway,
In harmony with nature's jest.
On this shore, we find our play,
In laughter's arms, we feel the rest.

Banter of the Bark and Breeze

The trees share glee through rustled leaves,
Echoing laughter, wise and old.
Barks of humor, no one grieves,
In nature's tale, new joys unfold.

A gentle gust whispers a joke,
Tickling branches with delight.
Every bark, it seems to poke,
At the sun, weaving in and out of sight.

Chattering leaves join in the fun,
While clouds drift by, they roll their eyes.
In this realm, joy has begun,
Painting smiles across the skies.

So lean on trees and feel their cheer,
As breezes carry chuckles near.
In every giggle, we grow clear,
Together we dance, with joy sincere.

Luminous Laughter in the Lap of Green

In the meadow, giggles spring,
Where daisies dance and children sing.
Bumblebees with hats so grand,
Tickle petals, play in hand.

A squirrel slips on acorn charm,
Spinning 'round, how sweet the harm.
Nature chuckles, skies ablaze,
As sunlight sets the world to gaze.

Laughter bubbles, breezes weave,
Joyful hearts, we can believe.
Grasshoppers jump in perfect sync,
While shadows play with thoughts to think.

All around, the fun's alive,
In this green, we dance and thrive.
Whispers of joy in every nook,
A storytime, a playful book.

The Levity of Sundrenched Spaces

Under rays of golden light,
Kites soar high, oh what a sight!
A cheeky breeze steals hats away,
While laughter spills, come join the play.

Frogs in tuxedos hop in pairs,
Making jokes without a care.
Butterflies, with colors bright,
Waltz through the warm, enchanted night.

Picnics spread with sandwiches,
Ants parade, the little whizz!
Giggling children chase the fun,
As shadows stretch, they start to run.

With every hint of sunny cheer,
Life's absurdities appear.
In these moments of blissful grace,
Joy and silliness interlace.

Whimsical Wonders That Bloom

Tulips wear their silly hats,
Bees play poker with the cats.
Sunflowers wink and take a peek,
At the antics, oh so cheek!

Rainbows laugh with colors bold,
Telling secrets, stories told.
Breezy whispers linger low,
With every chuckle, spirits flow.

Dandelions start a race,
Spreading giggles all over the place.
Pansies gossip, painting bright,
With each bloom, the world feels light.

In this garden, fun reigns supreme,
With every blossom, laughter beams.
Nature's jesters, wild and free,
Cradle joy—come dance with me.

The Frolic of the Feathered Flock

Birds in hats and polished shoes,
Strut about with funny views.
Wings that flap in comic glee,
Singing songs of jubilee.

Clouds of feathers fluff and spin,
With every tumble, we all win.
A parrot tells a joke so wide,
While all the finches laugh and glide.

In the trees, they share a jest,
With cuckoos joining, feeling blessed.
Each whistle brings a silly grin,
As chiming laughter starts to win.

Nature's chorus, light as air,
Brings a melody beyond compare.
Soaring high and feeling spry,
With these friends, we laugh and fly.

The Charm of Unruly Vines

In garden corners, folks do meet,
With tangled greens beneath their feet.
They whisper jokes, both sly and wise,
As winding branches wave and rise.

A squirrel darts, his acorn prize,
With nimble twirls and playful lies.
The sunlight dances, cast in glee,
Amongst the mischief, wild and free.

Petals laugh as breezes tease,
They sway and shimmy with such ease.
In this green chaos, joy does reign,
With every chuckle, we entertain.

So come and join this merry spree,
Where laughter blends with greenery.
Amidst the vines, with heart so bold,
The charm of whimsy never grows old.

Jubilant Journeys Along Nature's Lane

Through winding paths and shaded ways,
The trees share secrets of their days.
With every turn, a giggle found,
As nature's humor spins around.

A rabbit hops in silly bounds,
While birds exchange their sassy sounds.
Each flower nods with faces bright,
In this parade of pure delight.

The brook's soft chuckle adds a tune,
Inviting all beneath the moon.
With every step, a joyous shout,
As life and laughter dance about.

So stroll with me, let's lose track,
Of time and worries, we won't look back.
In nature's lane, let spirits soar,
With jubilant journeys, forevermore.

Flutters of Fun in the Foliage

In leafy realms where whispers play,
Tiny critters skitter away.
With winks and nods, they share a laugh,
Amidst the greens, they dance and craft.

The butterflies in bright array,
Perform their tricks in grand ballet.
Their colors bright, a vibrant show,
As laughter echoes, soft and low.

The bushes rustle with delight,
Where hidden giggles peek at night.
A charming ruckus, joyful sound,
In nature's heart, pure fun is found.

So come, my friend, embrace the glee,
In foliage where we're meant to be.
With flutters of fun, and spirits high,
Let every moment pass us by.

Vibrance of the Vineyard

In the vineyard, grapes do twirl,
Their laughter bounces, bright and pearled.
The sun tickles with rays so sweet,
As ants hold hands upon their feet.

A squirrel in a top hat prances,
While butterflies perform their dances.
The wine flows freely, jovial cheer,
As every sip uncorks a tear.

Grape jokes tumble from the vines,
A pun-filled harvest, oh how it shines!
With every toast, a giggle sends,
In this realm where mirth transcends.

A barrel rolls, a grape slips out,
It bounces high, we laugh and shout.
In nature's jest, we freely bask,
Atjoyful days, no need to mask.

Whimsy Among the Woods

In the heart of the playful grove,
A rabbit jests with tales he wove.
The trees giggle in the gentle breeze,
While mushrooms wear their hats with ease.

Squirrels debate what nuts to save,
With nutty puns, their hearts they brave.
A deer pranks fox, a dance they show,
In this funny forest, all joy flows.

The owls risk a silly scheme,
Winking eyes, a witty dream.
While fireflies jest, as night takes hold,
Their glowing jokes, a shimmer bold.

In whispering winds, laughter rings,
As nature draws us closer, sings.
With every step, we're quite bemused,
In this whimsical world, we're all amused.

Lyrical Lightheartedness

A feather floats from skies above,
Tickling thoughts like dreams of love.
With silly songs that dance in air,
We chase our cares, a joyous affair.

The clouds puff out like fluffy jokes,
While rainbows play as lively folks.
In every chuckle, delight we find,
As nature laughs, we're intertwined.

The river hums a merry tune,
While ducks parade, a waddle boon.
In sunny spots, the shadows tease,
We laugh aloud, our hearts at ease.

With every smile, we spin and sway,
A lightness guiding our play today.
In playful whispers of the breeze,
We gather joy like autumn leaves.

Revelry in the Roots

Down below where the fun begins,
The roots chuckle with secret sins.
They twist and shout beneath the ground,
In a laughter pact that knows no bound.

The worms tell tales of muddy slips,
While ants parade with tiny quips.
In this hidden world, a party thrives,
Where humor sprouts and joy arrives.

With every tangle, giggles grow,
As nature's smiles begin to show.
The soil hums a sprightly tune,
We join the revel under the moon.

In earthy jest, we find our feet,
Digging deep for laughter sweet.
The roots remind us, in their guise,
To embrace the joy that underlies.

Laughter Beneath the Boughs

In the shade where shadows play,
Squirrels dance, hip hip hooray!
A giggle from a tree so spry,
Twirling branches reach for the sky.

Beneath the boughs a prank unfolds,
Where whispers of mischief are told.
A frog in a crown, oh what a sight,
Belly laughs from morning till night.

Chirping birds join in the cheer,
Their joyful tunes are music dear.
A tickle from the breeze up high,
As butterflies flit and flutter by.

So take a seat, come join the fun,
Where laughter mingles with the sun.
Nature's jesters in vibrant hues,
Invite you to share in their views.

Echoes of Giggling Green

In a meadow where fairies play,
Laughter echoes, brightens the day.
Daisies chuckle as they sway,
Inviting all to join the fray.

A jolly deer with antics bold,
Stomps in rhythm, never cold.
Clip-clop shoes of a prancing goat,
Bringing joy with every note.

The wind tickles the timid streams,
Where fish jump high with giggling dreams.
A chorus of chuckles fills the air,
As nature's whimsy dances with flair.

So gather 'round, don't you be shy,
Let laughter soar, let spirits fly.
In the luscious green, joy takes wing,
With echoes of happiness flourishing.

Secrets in the Sunlit Canopy

High above where sunlight glows,
A whispering breeze, everyone knows.
The branches giggle in soft caress,
As secrets tumble in playful excess.

A wise old owl with a wink so sly,
Shares tales of joy that'll make you cry.
While playful raccoons, masks in place,
Join the jest with a grinning face.

Mushrooms smile beneath the trees,
Telling jokes on a floating breeze.
Laughter spills from nature's stage,
Turning each moment into a page.

So step beneath this bright expanse,
Where joy and humor lead the dance.
In the canopy, let merriment reign,
Secrets of joy will never wane.

Chasing Twinkles in the Air

Underneath the twinkling lights,
A troupe of critters hold delight.
Fireflies dress in sparkly flair,
As laughter dances through the air.

A cat with dreams of soaring high,
Takes leaps of faith, oh my, oh my!
With every hop, a giggle near,
As sparkles flicker, drawing cheer.

Across the field where shadows blend,
Happiness rolls, it has no end.
Tumbling leaves, a comedic sight,
Bringing chuckles on a soft night.

So let's chase twinkles, one and all,
With laughter as our curtain call.
In this joyful, luminous affair,
Find your giggles scattered everywhere.

Chortles in the Greenery

In the garden, giggles play,
Gnomes tiptoe on a sunny day.
Bees buzz-laughing in their flight,
Petals dance, oh, what a sight!

Squirrels chuckle up a tree,
Telling jokes to each marigold, you see.
Rabbits jump with gleeful cheer,
Swinging on the breeze so near!

Frogs in ponds croak silly tunes,
Tickling the air with their swoons.
A bounce, a hop, the joy expressed,
Nature's jest, we are all blessed!

Underneath this vibrant dome,
Laughter blossoms, makes us feel at home.
Gather 'round for fun galore,
In this green world, who could ask for more?

Sunbeams and Smiles

Sun shines bright with a wink and a grin,
Dancing shadows, shall we begin?
Ticklish rays upon our skin,
Gather round, let the fun spin!

Flowers beam in colors bold,
Waving secrets never told.
A giggle from a playful brook,
Brings smiles with just a little look.

Daisies whisper silly schemes,
Wishing on the sun's bright beams.
Each petal shimmers with delight,
Spreading joy from day to night.

In this bright and cheerful play,
Laughter leads us through the day.
Join the jubilee, don't be late,
In the warmth, we celebrate!

Echoes of Elation

Echoes ripple through the air,
Laughter floats without a care.
In the grove, the joy resounds,
Frolicking in merry bounds.

Whimsical tunes from chirping birds,
Tickle our hearts without words.
Breezes sprinkle giggles sweet,
Nature's humor, a delightful treat.

Caterpillars dance on leaves,
As if they wear festive sleeves.
Crickets join with evening songs,
Celebrating where joy belongs.

Underneath the moon's soft glow,
We embrace the laughter flow.
In every shadow, every gleam,
Echoes brighten our grand dream!

Colors of Cheer

Splashes of color, a joyful array,
Painting the world in a playful display.
Tulips twirl in swirls of fun,
Winking at the setting sun.

The sky wears its brightest blue,
While silly clouds drift, they poke through.
Butterflies flutter, flit, and tease,
Carefree spirits on the breeze.

Nature's palette, vivid and bright,
Each hue giggles in pure delight.
Glorious shades of joy emerge,
In this canvas, laughter will surge!

Join this rainbow on the run,
Embrace the joy that's just begun.
Together let's paint the scene,
With the colors of cheer, all serene!

Dappled Smiles on Emerald Paths

In the shade where shadows play,
Chasing giggles, bright and gay.
Wobbly walkers trip and tease,
Nature chuckles with the breeze.

Sunlight dapples on a grin,
Wiggles start where fun begins.
Footsteps dance on grassy floor,
Laughter echoes forevermore.

Whispers tumble through the trees,
Silly secrets on the breeze.
Jolly creatures jump and prance,
Inviting all to join the dance.

Paths of joy we cannot miss,
Every twist a giggle's bliss.
In this realm where jokes are spun,
Life is silly, life is fun.

Frothy Laughter of the Leafy Bower

Underneath the leafy shade,
Laughter's froth begins to parade.
Squirrels put on their best show,
Chasing tails in a comedic flow.

Tickling ferns and playful vines,
Gaze upon the joyful signs.
Here, the sunlight jests and jives,
In this haven, laughter thrives.

Bumbling bees in balmy air,
Buzzing jokes beyond compare.
Jolly shadows skip and sway,
In this bower, we'll laugh all day.

Every chuckle, sweet and light,
Transforms the day from dark to bright.
Beneath the blooms, we play and cheer,
Frothy laughter fills the atmosphere.

The Serendipity of the Swaying Branches

Wandering where the branches sway,
Discovering joy in play.
Twists of fate, a comic scene,
Life's a circus, bright and keen.

Branches bend with cheeky grins,
Leading us to playful sins.
Chuckles echo in the green,
In this realm of the unseen.

Swaying sprigs, a teasing breeze,
Silly moments, hearts at ease.
Every flip a burst of glee,
Nature's laughter sets us free.

In the dance of leaves and light,
Every tone feels just so right.
Serendipity leads the way,
As we laugh throughout the day.

Giggles in the Glorious Sunlight

Beneath the sun, the giggles rise,
Laughter's glow fills up the skies.
Dancing dandelions bloom,
Turning every gloom to fume.

Sunny rays create a cheer,
Sprightly joy is always near.
Wandering friends on shiny trails,
Telling stories, spinning tales.

Caterpillars in funny hats,
Join the fun with silly chats.
Chirp and chirp, the birds align,
Creating tunes to make us pine.

In this warmth, our spirits soar,
Each warm breeze, a joke to explore.
Giggles spill like sunlight bright,
In this world of pure delight.

Sunshine and Snickers

Beneath the bright and golden rays,
A squirrel dances, oh what a craze!
Chasing shadows with glee and style,
Stopping to giggle, every once in a while.

The daisies chuckle, in green array,
While butterflies twirl in their playful ballet.
The sun beams down with a cheeky grin,
As laughter bubbles from deep within.

Bumblebees buzz with a comical hum,
Tickling flowers, making them numb.
In this bright patch, joy is the key,
Sunshine and snickers for you and me!

Laughter echoes through skies so wide,
Nature's jesters, we take in our stride.
With each giggle, our spirits lift high,
In this sunny playground, we touch the sky.

The Joyful Rustle

In the breeze, leaves start to sing,
A playful chorus, nature's fling.
Whispers of mischief dance in the air,
Every rustling sound, a joke to share.

A cheeky robin hops with a wink,
While chipmunks plot and giggle, I think.
They chase each other in a comical race,
Frolicking freely, oh what a space!

The trees sway like they're laughing so hard,
Their branches jiggling, oh what a yard!
Nature's cackle fills the bright clear sky,
With every gust, more chuckles fly by.

In this joyful rustle, hilarity grows,
And the laughter in nature continuously flows.
Every moment, a jest we embrace,
In the heart of the woods, we find our grace.

Bursts of Bliss

A dandelion puff, oh what a sight,
Blowing gently, catching the light.
With each tender sneeze, a burst closes tight,
Sending giggles dancing into the night.

With every blossom, a chuckle is found,
As petals twirl softly upon the ground.
The bubbles of joy, released with a sigh,
In this garden of humor, we all just fly.

Nearby, a grasshopper hops with a cheer,
His leaps are like jokes that draw us near.
Tickled by laughter, we roll on the grass,
In the light of the sun, our troubles all pass.

Bursts of bliss fill the air like a song,
As we join in the laughter, it's where we belong.
In this playful haven, we dance and we sway,
Chasing the funny in the light of the day.

Nature's Comedy

The wind plays tricks, tickling the trees,
As critters collide, a tale of unease.
A raccoon stumbles in a hilarious spree,
While a nearby rabbit laughs back with glee.

The clouds turn shapes, like a whimsical mime,
Creating giggles in the warm afternoon time.
A cat on the porch watches with intrigue,
As the antics unfold, like silly fatigue.

With blossoms that wink and vines that tease,
Laughter echoed by buzzing bees.
Every sight is a jest, every sound a delight,
In this comedy of nature, joy takes flight.

So gather round, let your worries take flight,
Join in the giggles, it feels so right.
In this world of mirth, we find what we seek,
Nature's comedy is loud, never meek!

Happiness Hidden in the Bark

In the shadows where giggles sprout,
Beneath the surface, there's laughter about.
Squirrels dance with a mischievous flick,
Tickling the trees, a delightful trick.

Wrinkled old trunks with silly faces,
Whispering secrets in joyful places.
Chirping birds join in the festivity,
Creating a chorus of pure jestivity.

Roots rumble softly, a ticklish vibe,
As nature's humor starts to imbibe.
Each knot and twist tells a story bright,
Of frolicsome nights and pure daylight.

Underneath the canopy widely spread,
Lies a tapestry of laughter, finely threaded.
So come and listen, let your heart spark,
To the funny whispers, hidden in the bark.

The Vibrancy of Laughter's Leaves

In a world where giggles sway and twirl,
Every leaf dances, every petal's a pearl.
Colors burst forth in joyous parade,
Nature's grand jest, unashamedly played.

A breeze carries chuckles from high above,
While flowers wiggle, a show of love.
Bees buzzing hum their own silly tune,
As sunshine smiles down, bright as the moon.

In every petal hang stories so light,
Of humorous shadows that play in the night.
Giggles erupt from the ground to the air,
Frolicsome echoes that fill everywhere.

So join in the fun and let yourself be,
Part of this joy that is wild and free.
For in vibrant shades of laughter we find,
A life that is happy, carefree, and kind.

Cheerful Cadence of Petal and Wind

The wind whistles tunes through branches bare,
  Petals spin round, dancing without a care.
    Ruffling the grass with a playful sigh,
      As butterflies giggle and zoom on by.

  A waltz of the flowers, a jig in the sun,
Each colorful bloom knows how to have fun.
    Together they sway to an unseen beat,
      A circus of joy, so lively and sweet.

The clouds above chuckle, bursting with cheer,
  Painting the sky with laughter sincere.
    In every rustle, a secret is shared,
Of seasons and laughter, of moments declared.

So let's join the dance, with smiles we'll weave,
  In the cheerful cadence, we all can believe.
For beneath every petal and breeze that we feel,
  Lies the magic of laughter, so vivid and real.

Sway with the Glee of Green

In a grove where giggles bloom so bright,
Greenery winks under the warm sunlight.
Nature's humor wrapped in every twist,
Invites all to dance, you can't resist.

The grass chuckles beneath our bare feet,
A symphony swells, rhythmic and sweet.
Tiny critters join with their playful schemes,
Creating a world that bursts at the seams.

Every rustling leaf sings a funny song,
An anthem of joy where we all belong.
Swinging branches laugh at the clouds on high,
As rain drizzles down like a playful sigh.

So sway, oh dear friends, let laughter unwind,
In the embrace of green, joyfully blind.
For in nature's delight, our hearts shall gleam,
In the sway of the glee, we'll follow the dream.

Secrets Shared Under a Sapphire Sky

Beneath the wide, playful blue,
Whispers dance as giggles do.
A squirrel wears a tiny hat,
As clouds play coy, and cats go splat!

An ant tells jokes to passing ants,
The sunbeam twirls while nature prances.
A cheeky bird steals a slice of pie,
And on a whim, a tree sings why!

Breezes tickle the buzzing bees,
With laughter bright, they hum with ease.
A puppy trips, his ears a-flop,
In this realm, we never stop!

Secrets shared in nature's spree,
Under sapphire, wild and free.
With every bloom and joyful sight,
Giggles delight from day to night.

The Joyful Tangle of Nature's Croon

In the garden, a wild serenade,
Where butterflies flit in bright parade.
A jester frog leaps in a puddle,
Cracking jokes in a jovial huddle!

Among the vines, the laughter sneaks,
Each plant drums tunes as nature speaks.
A playful breeze tousles a bush,
And crickets join with a stifled hush.

A dandelion blows wishes wide,
With dreams and giggles on the tide.
A weasel winks, his tales sincere,
Nature's choir rings, so sweet to hear!

Joy entwined through each green twist,
In this glee, not a thing's amiss.
With nature's croon, come sway along,
In this jest-filled, playful throng!

Mirthful Murmurs in the Meadow

In a meadow filled with delight,
Bumbles buzz with pure delight.
A caterpillar spins a yarn,
While daisies chuckle, soft and warm.

The grasses giggle, swaying tall,
As raindrops tap a joyful call.
A grasshopper plays a light refrain,
With laughter in nature's grand domain.

A round old oak grins wide and bright,
Sharing secrets in the night.
With each soft breeze, the blossoms sway,
Encouraging smiles to bloom and play.

Mirthful murmurs, gentle tunes,
Beneath the watch of silver moons.
In every sound, a chuckle waits,
In the meadow, joy celebrates.

The Brightness of Giddy Gardens

In the garden where giggles sprout,
Colors laugh and dance about.
With flowers chatting, bright and bold,
Each petal whispers laughter told.

The pumpkins wear silly grins,
As harvest songs of fun begin.
Bees wear hats, a comical sight,
In this space of sheer delight!

The sun smiles down with golden rays,
Telling tales of happy days.
While rabbits hop in joyful bliss,
Each leap a chance not to miss!

The garden's heart, a spirited show,
Where laughter's bright and love will grow.
In giddy rays and playful sounds,
The brightness of joy eternally abounds.

The Lightheartedness of Greenery

In the park where giggles play,
The sunbeam dances day by day.
A squirrel spins with silly flair,
While daisies wink without a care.

A butterfly in polka dots,
Teases ants with silly plots.
Grasshoppers hop in comic spree,
As nature grins so joyfully.

A little frog with floppy feet,
Croaks a joke beneath the heat.
While flowers bloom with laughter bright,
Their petals sway in sheer delight.

So wander through this vibrant scene,
Where every shadow hides a dream.
With nature's charm, our smiles grow wide,
In this green world, we take a ride.

Jolly Encounters on the Trail

On paths where chuckles swirl and twirl,
Each step unveils a playful whirl.
A bouncing brook sings jovial tunes,
While playful pups chase glowing moons.

A cheerful bird on branches high,
Sings funny tales that flutter by.
While sunshine tickles ancient trees,
That sway and dance with every breeze.

A rabbit hops with comic grace,
Wearing a hat, a perfect place.
He winks and dashes, what a sight,
As all around him feels just right.

Through ticklish leaves and lifting sighs,
We laugh beneath the open skies.
On trails where joy and jest collide,
Adventure waits, let's take the ride!

A Symphony of Sprightly Sounds

In the meadow, laughter chimes,
As nature hums in joyful rhymes.
With buzzing bees that dance and twirl,
They serenade the swaying pearl.

A gentle breeze with playful grace,
Whistles tunes in leafy space.
While crickets chirp a late-night jest,
The fireflies blink, a bright-eyed fest.

A babbling brook, with jokes to share,
Splashes wit into the air.
As evening falls, the stars all wink,
In this laughter, we delightfully sink.

So listen close, the world unfolds,
Where every sound a tale beholds.
In this symphony, we take our stand,
With melodies that make us grand.

Cheerful Fronds and Whispered Winds

Fronds rejoice in gleeful flares,
With sunny grins and playful airs.
The whispering wind brings tales anew,
Of silly walks in morning dew.

A dandy dandelion puffs,
Spreading wishes, never gruffs.
While a giggling leaf skims the ground,
In this funny folly, joy is found.

Twirling trees with arms flung wide,
Embrace the skies, with spirits high.
They sway and shimmy, laughing free,
In this clumsy dance of jubilee.

So join the fun, let worries drift,
In nature's charm, we find our gift.
With cheerful fronds and breezy bends,
In laughter's heart, the journey blends.

www.ingramcontent.com/pod-product-compliance
Lightning Source LLC
Chambersburg PA
CBHW051630160426
43209CB00004B/588